THE LIFE YOU'RE MEANT TO LIVE

Paths To Purpose And Fulfillment

Thota Mahesh Babu

Title   : The Life You're Meant to Live: Paths to Purpose and Fulfillment

Author : Thota Mahesh Babu

Edition : First (July, 2024)

ISBN   : 9788197680816

Published by

TANEESHA PUBLISHERS | A Venture by -
PRACHI DIGITAL PUBLICATION

Regd. Add.: 254, Khuriyakhatta No. 10, Bindukhatta,
Lalkuan, Nainital - 262402, Uttarakhand, India
Website : www.taneeshapublishers.in
E-mail : taneeshapublishers@gmail.com
Phone : +91 845481 2712, +91 976041 7980

Printed by :
Manipal Technologies Limited, Bengaluru - 560001, Karnataka

Table of Content

Preface

Welcome, dear reader, to a journey of self-discovery, growth, and fulfillment. In the pages that follow, you'll embark on an exploration of the essential principles and practices that can help you cultivate a life of meaning, purpose, and joy.

Life is a magnificent tapestry, woven from the threads of our experiences, emotions, and aspirations. Yet, amidst the hustle and bustle of modern living, it's all too easy to lose sight of what truly matters—to become caught up in the relentless pursuit of success, wealth, and external validation, while neglecting the rich tapestry of our inner world.

This book is a gentle reminder to pause, reflect, and reconnect with the deepest truths of our being. It's a call to embrace change, cultivate resilience, and live with intention—to chart a course that aligns with our values, passions, and aspirations, rather than drifting aimlessly on the currents of circumstance.

Each chapter of this book delves into a different aspect of personal growth and fulfillment, offering insights, reflections, and practical exercises to support you on your journey. From embracing change and cultivating resilience to nurturing deep connections, pursuing passion, and finding balance in all areas of life, these pages are filled with wisdom drawn from ancient traditions, modern psychology, and the author's own lived experience.

But this book is more than just a collection of ideas—it's an invitation to embark on a transformative journey of self-discovery and self-mastery. It's an opportunity to explore the depths of your soul, uncover your true purpose, and unleash your full potential. It's a roadmap for living with greater awareness, authenticity, and aliveness, so that you may experience the richness and beauty of life in all its fullness.

As you navigate the chapters that follow, I encourage you to approach them with an open mind and an open heart. Take your time to reflect on the questions posed, engage with the exercises provided, and allow yourself to be fully present to the wisdom that emerges from within. And remember, the journey of personal growth is not a destination to be reached but a path to be walked—one step at a time, with courage, curiosity, and compassion.

May this book serve as a guiding light on your journey, illuminating the path ahead and inspiring you to live with greater purpose, passion, and presence. May it empower you to embrace change, cultivate resilience, and create a life that is deeply fulfilling and authentically yours.

With warmest regards,
Thota Mahesh Babu

Chapter 1

Introduction

Finding Your 'Why': The Importance of Discovering Your Purpose

In the vast tapestry of existence, each of us is a unique thread, woven with our own experiences, beliefs, and dreams. Yet, amid the chaos of everyday life, it's easy to lose sight of what truly makes us special. We find ourselves pondering a question that echoes through the ages: "What is my purpose?" This inquiry isn't just a philosophical musing; it's a beacon guiding us towards a life filled with meaning and significance.

Discovering your 'Why' is akin to finding your personal compass. It provides direction when life's path seems uncertain, infuses your actions with purpose during challenging times, and adds depth and meaning to your everyday existence. Your 'Why' isn't merely about setting lofty goals; it's about aligning your daily choices with your deepest values and passions. It transforms mundane moments into opportunities for growth and contribution, making each day feel like a step towards something greater.

As we embark on this journey of self-discovery, it's essential to remember the words of Mark Twain: "The two most important days in your life are the day you are born and the day you find out why." Finding your 'Why' isn't a one-time event; it's an ongoing process of introspection and reflection. It requires a willingness to explore the depths of your soul, to uncover the driving forces behind your actions and aspirations.

Consider the story of Sarah, a woman who seemed to have it all — a successful career, a loving family, and financial stability. Yet, despite outward appearances, Sarah felt a nagging sense of emptiness. It wasn't until she took the time to delve into her own motivations and desires that she discovered her true purpose: to make a positive impact on the lives of others through mentorship and coaching. With this newfound clarity, Sarah's life took on a new sense of meaning and fulfillment, guiding her towards a path aligned with her deepest values.

Our 'Why' isn't something static; it evolves and grows as we do. It's a reflection of our ever-changing desires, passions, and aspirations. By continually revisiting and refining our understanding of our 'Why,' we can ensure that our actions remain in alignment with our deepest values and aspirations.

As we navigate the journey of self-discovery, let us remember the words of Buddha: "Your purpose in life is to find your purpose and give your whole heart and soul to it." Finding your 'Why' isn't always easy, but it's a journey worth embarking on. It's about embracing the uniqueness of who you are and living a life that feels authentic and fulfilling.

In the end, our 'Why' is what gives our lives meaning and purpose. It's the guiding force that helps us navigate life's ups and downs with grace and resilience. So, let us embrace the journey of self-discovery wholeheartedly, knowing that by uncovering our 'Why,' we can live a life that is truly meaningful and fulfilling.

The Journey Ahead: Overview of the Book's Aims and How to Use It

"The Life You're Meant to Live: Paths to Purpose and Fulfilment" beckons you to embark on a profound journey of self-discovery and personal growth. Within its pages lie invaluable insights and practical guidance, each chapter serving as a stepping stone along the path toward understanding yourself and crafting a life that resonates with your true essence. Through exploration of topics such as mindfulness, well-being, passion, resilience, and happiness, this book seeks to illuminate the way toward a life of deeper meaning and satisfaction.

At its core, this book is both a mirror and a map. It acts as a mirror, reflecting back to you the truths you may have overlooked about yourself and your potential. Through introspective exercises and thought-provoking questions, it invites you to gaze inward and uncover the hidden depths of your being. But it is also a map, providing clear routes and guidance on how to navigate the terrain of self-discovery and personal growth. Each chapter offers insights, practical advice, and actionable steps, guiding you toward a life that aligns with your deepest values and aspirations.

To truly benefit from this journey, active engagement is key. I encourage you to immerse yourself fully in the exploration laid out before you. Take the time to reflect on the questions posed, journal your thoughts and insights, and implement the practices suggested. Remember, transformation is a process, not a destination. Every step you take, no matter how small, brings you closer to the life you aspire to live.

As we embark on this journey together, it's important to acknowledge that the path to discovering your 'Why' and living a fulfilling life is uniquely yours. While this book serves as a guide, the choices, changes, and commitments you make are what will ultimately shape your destiny. You are the author of your own story, and this book is merely a tool to help you uncover the chapters waiting to be written.

In the words of poet Rumi, "The journey of a thousand miles begins with a single step." Let this book be your companion as you take those first steps toward a life of purpose and fulfilment. Welcome to "The Life You're Meant to Live." Together, let us embark on this adventure with open hearts and minds, ready to explore the vast potentials within us and the beautiful possibilities that lie ahead.

Chapter 2

Finding Your 'Why': The Importance of Discovering Your Purpose

Discovering your 'Why' is like uncovering a hidden treasure within yourself. It's about finding the reason you get up in the morning, beyond just going to work or completing daily tasks. This journey to uncover your purpose is the most crucial step you'll take because it shapes everything you do, think, and feel. It's your guiding star in the vast sky of life, helping you navigate through both smooth and rough waters.

"Your 'Why' gives you clarity," as Simon Sinek famously said, "People don't buy what you do; they buy why you do it." While Sinek refers to businesses, this idea is profoundly true for individuals as well. Knowing your 'Why' brings clarity to your actions and attracts people and opportunities that align with your values. It's not about impressing others but about being authentically you, which in turn lights the path to a more fulfilling life.

Imagine waking up each day with a clear sense of purpose. This doesn't mean you won't face challenges or moments of doubt, but with your 'Why' firmly in your heart, you'll have the strength to overcome them. As Friedrich Nietzsche once said, "He who has a why to live can bear almost any how." This powerful statement reminds us that when we know our purpose, we can endure hardships, find solutions to problems, and stay focused on our goals, no matter how tough the journey gets.

Finding your 'Why' requires deep self-reflection. It's about asking yourself what truly makes you happy, what you're passionate about, and what you want your legacy to be. It's not an overnight process, and for many, it's a path filled with questions. But remember, as Rumi beautifully put it, "What you seek is seeking you." This means your purpose is out there, aligning with your passions and strengths, waiting to be discovered.

Consider the story of individuals who've left a mark on the world by following their 'Why.' Think of Martin Luther King Jr., who was driven by a vision of equality and love, or Mother Teresa, who found her purpose in serving the poor and the sick. Their 'Whys' were clear, propelling them forward, inspiring others, and making a significant impact. Their lives exemplify how understanding and pursuing your purpose can lead to not just personal fulfillment but also to the betterment of society.

Your 'Why' evolves with you. It's shaped by your experiences, beliefs, and dreams. As you grow and change, so might your purpose. This is perfectly normal. The key is to stay in tune with your inner self, to continuously explore what brings you joy, satisfaction, and a sense of achievement.

To embark on this journey of discovering your 'Why,' start by setting aside quiet time for reflection. Think about moments in your life when you felt most alive, most excited, and most proud. What were you doing? Who were you with? These moments can offer clues to your true purpose. Additionally, consider what you can do that combines your talents and passions in a way that serves others. As Arthur Ashe famously said, "Success is a journey, not a destination. The doing is often more important than the outcome." This is especially true when it comes to finding your 'Why.' It's about the journey, the learning, and the growth that comes from exploring what makes you uniquely you.

Journaling your thoughts and feelings can be a powerful tool in this process. Writing down your reflections can help clarify your thoughts and highlight patterns or themes in your life that point towards your purpose. It's also beneficial to talk about your search for purpose with trusted friends or mentors. Sometimes, an outside perspective can offer insights that you might overlook.

In finding your 'Why,' you unlock the door to a more passionate, satisfying, and meaningful life. It's the difference between just existing and truly living. As Mark Twain once noted, "The two most important days in your life are the day you are born and the day you find out why." Discovering your purpose is akin to finding your place in the world, a sense of belonging and direction that guides your choices and actions.

In conclusion, embarking on the journey to discover your 'Why' is perhaps the most important adventure you will undertake. It shapes your decisions, influences your actions, and defines your path in life. Your 'Why' is your heart's deepest desire, the core of who you are and what you wish to contribute to the world. It's about living authentically, pursuing your passions, and making a difference. Remember, the pursuit of your 'Why' is a journey marked by self-discovery, growth, and transformation. Embrace it wholeheartedly, for it is the path to a truly fulfilling life.

Chapter 3

The Art of Embracing Change

Change. It's the one constant in life, an ever-present force shaping our experiences, challenging our beliefs, and pushing us out of our comfort zones. Yet, despite its inevitability, change often evokes feelings of fear, uncertainty, and resistance. In this chapter, we'll explore the art of embracing change as not just a necessity of life, but as a powerful catalyst for growth, transformation, and personal evolution.

Change can take many forms – from small shifts in our daily routines to major life transitions that alter the course of our existence. Whether it's a new job, a relationship ending, a move to a new city, or a global pandemic reshaping the world as we know it, change forces us to adapt, to let go of what was and embrace what is to come.

So how do we navigate the turbulent waters of change with grace and resilience? How do we shift our perspective from one of fear and resistance to one of acceptance and opportunity? The answer lies in cultivating a mindset that sees change not as a threat, but as a doorway to growth and transformation.

One of the first steps in embracing change is to recognize and accept its inevitability. Change is a natural part of the human experience, an integral aspect of our journey through life. Instead of resisting or fearing change, we can choose to acknowledge its presence, to greet it with an open heart and an open mind.

Next, we can practice flexibility and adaptability in the face of change. Like the branches of a tree swaying in the wind, we can learn to bend without breaking, to adjust our sails when the winds of change blow us off course. This means letting go of rigid expectations and embracing the uncertainty that comes with change, trusting that we have the inner resources and resilience to navigate whatever comes our way.

Another powerful strategy for embracing change is to reframe our perspective. Instead of viewing change as a threat, we can see it as an opportunity for growth, learning, and self-discovery. Every change, no matter how difficult or unexpected, carries with it the potential for transformation. By shifting our focus from what we're losing to what we're gaining, from what's ending to what's beginning, we can approach change with a sense of curiosity and excitement rather than fear and resistance.

Moreover, we can cultivate a sense of gratitude for the opportunities that change brings into our lives. Even in the midst of uncertainty and upheaval, there is always something to be thankful for – whether it's the chance to start anew, the lessons learned through adversity, or the strength and resilience that emerge from facing challenges head-on. By practicing gratitude, we can find beauty and meaning in even the most difficult of circumstances, turning moments of change into opportunities for growth and self-discovery.

Finally, we can lean on our support networks during times of change. Whether it's friends, family, mentors, or counselors, having a strong support system can provide comfort, guidance, and reassurance as we navigate the ups and downs of life's transitions. By reaching out and connecting with others, we remind ourselves that we are not alone in our journey, that there are people who care about us and are there to help us through even the toughest of times.

In conclusion, the art of embracing change is not about avoiding or resisting the inevitable shifts and transitions of life, but about meeting them with courage, resilience, and an open heart. By acknowledging the inevitability of change, practicing flexibility and adaptability, reframing our perspective, cultivating gratitude, and leaning on our support networks, we can navigate the ever-changing landscape of life with grace and resilience. And in doing so, we open ourselves up to the endless possibilities for growth, transformation, and personal evolution that change brings into our lives.

Chapter 4

Cultivating Resilience in the Face of Adversity

Life is not always smooth sailing. Along our journey, we encounter storms—challenges, setbacks, and hardships that test our strength and resilience. In the face of adversity, it's easy to feel overwhelmed, defeated, and powerless. But it is precisely during these difficult times that our resilience is put to the test.

Resilience is the ability to bounce back from adversity—to adapt, grow, and thrive in the face of life's challenges. It is not about avoiding difficulties or denying their existence but rather about facing them head-on with strength, courage, and grace. As the Japanese proverb says, "Fall seven times, stand up eight."

Cultivating resilience begins with acknowledging the reality of our circumstances—accepting that adversity is a natural part of life and that we cannot always control the events that unfold around us. It is about adopting a mindset of acceptance and surrender, recognizing that while we may not be able to change our circumstances, we can choose how we respond to them. As Viktor Frankl famously wrote, "When we are no longer able to change a situation, we are challenged to change ourselves."

One of the key components of resilience is self-awareness—understanding our own strengths, weaknesses, and coping mechanisms. By knowing ourselves deeply, we can better navigate through adversity and tap into our inner reservoirs of strength and resilience. This self-awareness allows us to identify potential triggers, recognize when we are feeling overwhelmed, and implement strategies to help us cope effectively.

Another essential aspect of resilience is maintaining a positive outlook—even in the face of adversity. This does not mean denying the reality of our circumstances or putting on a false sense of optimism but rather choosing to focus on the opportunities for growth and learning that adversity presents. As Helen Keller once said, "Although the world is full of suffering, it is also full of the overcoming of it."

Practicing gratitude is a powerful tool for building resilience, as it helps us shift our focus from what is lacking to what is abundant in our lives. By cultivating a daily practice of gratitude, we train our minds to see the silver linings amidst the storm clouds—to find beauty, joy, and meaning even in the midst of adversity. As Melody Beattie wrote, "Gratitude unlocks the fullness of life. It turns what we have into enough and more."

Resilience also involves seeking support from others—leaning on friends, family, and community for encouragement, guidance, and emotional support. It is important to remember that we do not have to face adversity alone—that there is strength in vulnerability and power in connection. As Brene Brown famously said, "Vulnerability is not weakness; it's our greatest measure of courage."

In addition to seeking support from others, it is essential to practice self-care during times of adversity. This means prioritizing our physical, emotional, and mental well-being—eating nourishing foods, getting enough rest, engaging in activities that bring us joy, and seeking professional help if needed. Self-care is not selfish—it is a necessary investment in our resilience and well-being.

Finally, resilience is about embracing the lessons that adversity has to offer—to find meaning, purpose, and growth in the midst of our struggles. It is about recognizing that even the darkest of times can be catalysts for transformation and renewal. As Friedrich Nietzsche wrote,

"That which does not kill us makes us stronger."

In conclusion, cultivating resilience is essential for navigating through life's challenges with strength, courage, and grace. It is about embracing adversity as an opportunity for growth, learning, and self-discovery. By practicing self-awareness, maintaining a positive outlook, seeking support, practicing gratitude, and embracing the lessons of adversity, we can cultivate resilience and emerge from life's storms stronger, wiser, and more resilient than ever before. As Maya Angelou famously said, "You may encounter many defeats, but you must not be defeated. In fact, it may be necessary to encounter the defeats, so you can know who you are, what you can rise from, how you can still come out of it."

Chapter 5

Unlocking the Power of Mindfulness

In the chaos of modern life, our minds often race from one thought to the next, dwelling on the past or worrying about the future, rarely fully present in the here and now. It's amidst this whirlwind of distractions that mindfulness emerges as a beacon of tranquility, offering us a pathway to inner peace and contentment. In this chapter, we'll delve into the transformative practice of mindfulness and explore its profound power to cultivate present-moment awareness, leading us to deeper contentment and peace.

At its core, mindfulness is simply the practice of being fully present in the present moment, without judgment or attachment to thoughts or emotions. It's about bringing our attention to the here and now, noticing our thoughts, feelings, and sensations as they arise, and allowing them to pass without getting caught up in them.

Mindfulness invites us to observe our inner experiences with curiosity and compassion, cultivating a sense of acceptance and non-reactivity to whatever arises within us.

One of the foundational aspects of mindfulness is conscious breathing. By bringing our awareness to the sensation of our breath as it flows in and out of our bodies, we anchor ourselves in the present moment, grounding ourselves in the here and now. With each breath, we let go of the past and the future, coming home to the present moment with a sense of peace and clarity.

Mindfulness also involves paying attention to our senses, fully engaging with the sights, sounds, smells, tastes, and tactile sensations of our immediate environment. Whether it's feeling the warmth of the sun on our skin, listening to the sound of birdsong, or savoring the taste of a delicious meal, mindfulness invites us to fully immerse ourselves in the richness of our sensory experience, awakening us to the beauty and wonder of the present moment.

Another key aspect of mindfulness is cultivating awareness of our thoughts and emotions. Instead of getting swept away by the endless stream of thoughts that pass through our minds or reacting impulsively to our emotions, mindfulness teaches us to observe them with curiosity and compassion. We learn to recognize that our thoughts are not facts, our emotions are not our identities, and that we have the power to choose how we respond to them in each moment.

Through the practice of mindfulness, we develop greater emotional resilience and self-regulation, allowing us to respond to life's challenges with calmness and clarity rather than reactively. We become less entangled in the grip of our fears, anxieties, and worries, and more able to navigate life's ups and downs with grace and equanimity.

Moreover, mindfulness has been scientifically proven to have numerous physical and mental health benefits. From reducing stress and anxiety to improving sleep quality and enhancing immune function, mindfulness has the power to positively impact every aspect of our well-being. By regularly incorporating mindfulness practices into our daily lives, we can cultivate greater resilience, vitality, and overall happiness.

In conclusion, mindfulness is a profound tool for unlocking the power of the present moment, leading us to deeper contentment and peace in our lives. By cultivating present-moment awareness, practicing conscious breathing, engaging fully with our senses, and observing our thoughts and emotions with curiosity and compassion, we can awaken to the richness and beauty of each moment. And in doing so, we discover a profound sense of inner peace, joy, and contentment that transcends the chaos of the external world.

Chapter 6

Nurturing Deep Connections

In the tapestry of our lives, relationships form the threads that weave together our experiences, shaping who we are and how we navigate the world. Deep connections with others are essential for our emotional well-being, sense of belonging, and overall happiness. In this chapter, we explore the profound importance of relationships and offer insights into cultivating meaningful connections with others.

At its essence, nurturing deep connections is about fostering genuine intimacy, trust, and mutual support in our relationships. It's about creating spaces where we can show up authentically, be seen and heard without judgment, and feel valued and accepted for who we truly are. As Brené Brown beautifully expresses it, "Connection is the energy that exists between people when they feel seen, heard, and valued; when they can give and receive without judgment; and when they derive sustenance and strength from the relationship."

One of the foundations of nurturing deep connections is effective communication. Communication is not just about exchanging words—it's about truly listening to understand, expressing ourselves honestly and compassionately, and being fully present with others. By practicing active listening, empathy, and nonjudgmental presence, we create spaces for deeper connection and understanding in our relationships.

Vulnerability is another essential component of nurturing deep connections. It is the willingness to show up authentically, share our true thoughts and feelings, and open ourselves up to the possibility of being seen and accepted for who we are. While vulnerability can feel uncomfortable and scary at times, it is the gateway to intimacy and connection. As Brené Brown reminds us, "Vulnerability is the birthplace of love, belonging, joy, courage, empathy, and creativity."

Trust is the bedrock of any meaningful relationship. It is built over time through consistency, honesty, and integrity in our words and actions. Trust allows us to feel safe and secure in our connections with others, knowing that we can rely on them for support, understanding, and acceptance. As Ralph Waldo Emerson said, "The glory of friendship is not the outstretched hand, not the kindly smile, nor the joy of companionship; it is the spiritual inspiration that comes to one when you discover that someone else believes in you and is willing to trust you with a friendship."

Empathy is the ability to step into another person's shoes, to understand their thoughts, feelings, and experiences from their perspective. It is the foundation of compassion and connection in our relationships, allowing us to bridge the gap between our differences and cultivate deeper understanding and intimacy. As Carl Rogers famously said, "When someone really hears you without passing judgment on you, without trying to take responsibility for you, without trying to mold you, it feels damn good."

In addition to effective communication, vulnerability, trust, and empathy, nurturing deep connections also requires time, effort, and commitment. It involves prioritizing our relationships, making time for meaningful conversations and shared experiences, and showing up consistently with presence, kindness, and authenticity. By investing in our relationships in this way, we can create bonds that are resilient, nurturing, and deeply fulfilling.

In conclusion, nurturing deep connections is essential for our emotional well-being, sense of belonging, and overall happiness. By fostering effective communication, vulnerability, trust, and empathy in our relationships, we can create spaces where we feel seen, heard, and valued for who we truly are. As Maya Angelou beautifully expresses it, "I've learned that people will forget what you said, people will forget what you did, but people will never forget how you made them feel."

Chapter 7

The Pursuit of Passion and Creativity

In the tapestry of our lives, passion and creativity are the vibrant threads that add depth, color, and meaning to the canvas of our existence. They are the fuel that ignites our souls, propelling us forward on a journey of self-discovery, growth, and fulfillment. In this chapter, we embark on an exploration of the profound importance of pursuing our passions and nurturing our creativity as essential pathways to joy and fulfillment.

Passion is the fire that burns within us, driving us to pursue the things that excite us, inspire us, and fill us with a sense of purpose and meaning. It's the spark of enthusiasm that propels us out of bed in the morning, eager to immerse ourselves in activities that energize and fulfill us. Whether it's painting, writing, dancing, gardening, or any other pursuit that sets our hearts ablaze, passion is the fuel that sustains our journey and infuses every moment with vitality and joy.

But passion alone is not enough; it must be coupled with creativity—the ability to think outside the box, to imagine new possibilities, and to express ourselves authentically. Creativity is the alchemical process through which we transform our passions into works of art, whether tangible or intangible, that reflect our unique perspectives and experiences. It's the act of turning inspiration into innovation, of bringing something new and beautiful into the world through our thoughts, words, and actions.

Yet, despite the inherent importance of passion and creativity in our lives, many of us suppress or neglect these vital aspects of our being out of fear, self-doubt, or societal pressures. We may believe that we're not talented enough, that our passions are frivolous, or that we're too busy to pursue them. But in doing so, we deny ourselves the opportunity to experience the deep sense of joy, fulfillment, and aliveness that comes from living authentically and wholeheartedly.

So how do we reconnect with our passions and unleash our creativity? It begins with self-discovery—taking the time to explore our interests, values, and desires, and identifying the activities that truly light us up from within. It's about listening to the whispers of our hearts, honoring our inner callings, and giving ourselves permission to pursue the things that bring us joy and fulfillment, regardless of external expectations or judgments.

Once we've identified our passions, the next step is to cultivate them— to devote time, energy, and attention to nurturing our interests and expanding our creative horizons. This may involve setting aside dedicated time for creative pursuits, seeking out opportunities for learning and growth, and surrounding ourselves with people who support and encourage our creative endeavors. It's about making a commitment to ourselves and our dreams, and taking deliberate action to bring them to fruition.

Moreover, embracing passion and creativity in our lives not only brings us personal fulfillment but also enriches the world around us. When we express ourselves authentically and share our gifts with others, we inspire those around us to do the same. We create ripple effects of joy, inspiration, and transformation that extend far beyond ourselves, touching the lives of others in ways we may never fully realize.

In conclusion, the pursuit of passion and creativity is not just a luxury— it's a fundamental aspect of what it means to be human. By reconnecting with our passions, nurturing our creativity, and expressing ourselves authentically, we tap into a deep wellspring of joy, fulfillment, and aliveness that enriches every aspect of our lives. So let us embrace our passions, unleash our creativity, and embark on a journey of self-discovery and self-expression that leads us to greater joy, meaning, and purpose.

Chapter 8

Embracing Authenticity

Authenticity is the cornerstone of a meaningful and fulfilling life—it is the art of being true to oneself, embracing our uniqueness, and living in alignment with our deepest values and aspirations. In this chapter, we delve into the importance of authenticity and the liberation that comes from self-acceptance.

Living authentically means honoring our true selves—the unfiltered essence of who we are—without pretense or masks. It requires the courage to show up as our genuine selves, even when it's uncomfortable or challenging. As Dr. Seuss famously said, "Today you are You, that is truer than true. There is no one alive who is Youer than You."

Embracing authenticity involves letting go of the need for approval or validation from others and trusting in our own inner guidance. It means listening to the whispers of our hearts and honoring the unique path that calls to us, even if it diverges from societal expectations or norms. As Ralph Waldo Emerson wrote, "To be yourself in a world that is constantly trying to make you something else is the greatest accomplishment."

Self-acceptance is the foundation of authenticity—it is the radical act of embracing ourselves exactly as we are, flaws and all. It requires compassion, kindness, and forgiveness toward ourselves, recognizing that our worthiness is inherent and unconditional. As Brene Brown beautifully expresses it, "Authenticity is the daily practice of letting go of who we think we're supposed to be and embracing who we are."

Authenticity is not about being perfect or having it all together—it's about embracing our imperfections and vulnerabilities as integral parts of our humanity. It's about being honest with ourselves and others, even when it's uncomfortable or scary. As Maya Angelou famously said, "I did then what I knew how to do. Now that I know better, I do better."

Living authentically is a journey of self-discovery, self-expression, and self-empowerment. It involves embracing our passions, values, and dreams wholeheartedly, and letting go of the fear of judgment or rejection. As Oscar Wilde wrote, "Be yourself; everyone else is already taken."

In conclusion, embracing authenticity is the key to living a life of purpose, fulfillment, and joy. When we honor our true selves, we create space for meaningful connections, creative expression, and personal growth. As we journey inward to discover our authentic selves, we unleash the power of our unique gifts and talents, and inspire others to do the same. As Marianne Williamson famously said, "As we let our own light shine, we unconsciously give other people permission to do the same. As we are liberated from our own fear, our presence automatically liberates others."

Chapter 9

Overcoming Fear and Doubt

In the grand theater of life, fear and doubt often take center stage, casting shadows over our aspirations and dreams. Yet, within the depths of our souls, lies the courage to confront these adversaries and emerge victorious. This chapter is a guide—an anthem—to overcoming fear and doubt, unlocking the door to a life lived freely and fully.

Fear, like a shadow, follows us wherever we go, whispering tales of uncertainty and limitation. But within every shadow lies the potential for light to dispel darkness. Embrace fear not as a foe, but as a companion on the journey toward growth. Let it be the catalyst that propels you forward, rather than the anchor that holds you back.

Doubt, with its nagging whispers of inadequacy, seeks to erode our confidence and stifle our dreams. Yet, within the quiet chambers of our hearts, lies the unwavering belief in our own worthiness and potential. Silence the voice of doubt with the roar of determination, knowing that you are capable of achieving greatness beyond measure.

In the face of fear and doubt, resilience becomes our greatest ally—a shining beacon of hope in the midst of uncertainty. Cultivate resilience not by avoiding challenges, but by confronting them head-on with unwavering resolve. Let every setback be a stepping stone toward greater strength and self-discovery.

Forge ahead with courage, knowing that the path to success is paved with obstacles overcome and fears conquered. Embrace failure not as a defeat, but as a lesson in resilience and perseverance. As you navigate the twists and turns of life's journey, remember that every setback is an opportunity for growth and transformation.

Believe in yourself with unwavering conviction, knowing that you possess the power to overcome any obstacle that stands in your way. Trust in your abilities, and let your inner light shine brightly, illuminating the path forward with clarity and purpose.

In conclusion, overcoming fear and doubt is not a destination, but a journey—an ongoing process of growth and self-discovery. Embrace the challenges that lie ahead with courage and determination, knowing that you are capable of achieving greatness beyond your wildest dreams. As you step boldly into the unknown, remember these words: "Fear may knock at the door of your heart, but courage will always answer."

Chapter 10

Cultivating a Growth Mindset

In the garden of personal development, the seeds of a growth mindset bloom into the flowers of resilience, adaptability, and lifelong learning. This chapter is a journey into the fertile soil of the mind—a call to cultivate a mindset that thrives on challenges, embraces failure as a stepping stone to success, and celebrates the journey of continual growth and improvement.

At the heart of a growth mindset lies the belief that our abilities and intelligence can be developed through dedication and hard work. Instead of seeing challenges as insurmountable obstacles, individuals with a growth mindset view them as opportunities for growth and learning. Like a gardener tending to their plants, they nurture their skills and talents with perseverance and determination, knowing that with effort and practice, anything is possible.

Adaptability is the cornerstone of a growth mindset—it is the ability to flex and bend in the face of adversity, to embrace change as a natural part of life's journey. Rather than resisting change, those with a growth mindset welcome it with open arms, knowing that it offers new opportunities for growth and self-discovery. Like a tree swaying in the wind, they bend but never break, resilient in the face of life's storms.

Failure is not a stumbling block for those with a growth mindset, but rather a stepping stone on the path to success. Instead of viewing failure as a reflection of their abilities, they see it as an opportunity to learn, grow, and improve. Like a phoenix rising from the ashes, they emerge stronger and more determined than ever, ready to tackle the challenges that lie ahead.

In the garden of the mind, the soil of a growth mindset is enriched by curiosity, passion, and a thirst for knowledge. Those who cultivate a growth mindset approach life with a sense of wonder and curiosity, eager to explore new ideas and perspectives. They see setbacks not as failures, but as opportunities for discovery and growth. Like a perennial plant that blooms year after year, their potential knows no bounds.

In conclusion, cultivating a growth mindset is not just about developing skills or achieving success—it's about embracing the journey of continual growth and improvement. It's about seeing challenges as opportunities, failure as feedback, and change as a catalyst for personal transformation. As you nurture the seeds of a growth mindset within yourself, remember these words: "The only limit to your growth is the extent of your imagination and the depth of your determination."

Chapter 11

The Power of Gratitude

In the symphony of life, gratitude is the melody that uplifts the soul and fills the heart with joy. This chapter is a celebration—a hymn—to the transformative power of gratitude, a practice that has the ability to shift our perspective, enhance our well-being, and attract positivity into our lives.

At its core, gratitude is a state of mind—a way of seeing the world through the lens of appreciation and abundance. Instead of focusing on what we lack, gratitude invites us to acknowledge and cherish the blessings that surround us each day. Like a beacon of light in the darkness, it illuminates the beauty and wonder that often go unnoticed in our busy lives.

Practicing gratitude is like tending to a garden—each day, we plant seeds of thankfulness and watch as they grow and flourish. By consciously cultivating an attitude of gratitude, we train our minds to seek out the good in every situation, no matter how challenging or difficult. Like a flower turning its face toward the sun, gratitude helps us find beauty and joy even in the midst of adversity.

The benefits of gratitude extend far beyond mere positivity—it has been scientifically proven to enhance our physical and mental well-being. Studies have shown that gratitude can strengthen our immune system, lower our blood pressure, and improve our sleep quality. It also has profound effects on our mental health, reducing symptoms of depression and anxiety, and increasing feelings of happiness and contentment.

But perhaps the most powerful aspect of gratitude is its ability to attract positivity into our lives. Like a magnet, gratitude draws to us more of what we focus on, creating a virtuous cycle of abundance and joy. When we express gratitude for the blessings we already have, we open ourselves up to receiving even more blessings in return. It's a simple yet profound truth—what we appreciate, appreciates.

In conclusion, the power of gratitude lies not in grand gestures or elaborate rituals, but in the simple act of acknowledging and appreciating the abundance that surrounds us each day. As you embark on your own journey of gratitude, remember these words: "Gratitude unlocks the fullness of life. It turns what we have into enough, and more. It turns denial into acceptance, chaos into order, confusion into clarity. It can turn a meal into a feast, a house into a home, a stranger into a friend."

Chapter 12

Living with Intention

In the tapestry of existence, living with intention is the thread that weaves purpose and meaning into the fabric of our lives. This chapter is an invitation—a call—to embrace the power of intentionality, to make conscious choices, set clear intentions, and align our actions with our deepest values for a life of purpose and fulfillment.

Living with intention is about more than just going through the motions—it's about consciously directing the course of our lives, moment by moment, choice by choice. It's about pausing to consider what truly matters to us, and then taking deliberate action to bring those values into alignment with our everyday actions. Like a sculptor shaping clay, living with intention allows us to mold our lives according to our highest aspirations.

Setting intentions is the first step on the path to living with purpose. By clarifying our intentions, we create a roadmap for our lives—a guiding light that illuminates our path and keeps us focused on what truly matters. Whether it's cultivating deeper relationships, pursuing a passion, or making a positive impact in the world, setting clear intentions empowers us to live with clarity, direction, and purpose.

Making conscious choices is the next crucial step in living with intention. Instead of allowing life to happen to us, we take an active role in shaping our destiny by making choices that align with our values and aspirations. Like a captain navigating a ship through stormy seas, we steer our lives in the direction of our dreams, always mindful of the choices we make along the way.

Aligning our actions with our values is the final piece of the puzzle. It's one thing to set intentions and make conscious choices, but it's another thing entirely to follow through with action. Living with intention requires us to walk the talk—to embody our values in everything we do, from the smallest daily tasks to the grandest life decisions. Like a tree rooted firmly in the earth, living with intention grounds us in our values and gives us the strength to weather life's storms with grace and resilience.

In conclusion, living with intention is a powerful practice that empowers us to live with purpose, clarity, and authenticity. As you embark on your own journey of intentionality, remember these words: "The secret of your future is hidden in your daily routine. What you do today can shape the course of your life tomorrow." By setting clear intentions, making conscious choices, and aligning your actions with your values, you can create a life that is rich in meaning, purpose, and fulfillment.

Chapter 13

Finding Balance: Work, Life and Play

In the bustling rhythm of modern life, finding balance is the gentle dance between responsibilities and pleasures—a delicate equilibrium that nourishes the soul and rejuvenates the spirit. This chapter is a sanctuary—a refuge—for those seeking to harmonize the demands of work, personal life, and leisure, while embracing the vital importance of self-care and rest.

Balance is not a static state to be achieved, but rather a dynamic process of constant adjustment and recalibration. Like a tightrope walker navigating the taut line between two poles, finding balance requires mindfulness, flexibility, and grace. It's about recognizing when to lean in and when to step back, when to exert effort and when to surrender to the flow of life.

Achieving balance begins with prioritizing self-care—the cornerstone upon which all else rests. Just as a gardener tends to the needs of the soil before planting seeds, we must nourish our bodies, minds, and spirits to thrive in all areas of our lives. This means making time for rest, relaxation, and rejuvenation, as well as engaging in activities that bring us joy and fulfillment. Like a wellspring of vitality, self-care replenishes our reserves and empowers us to meet life's challenges with resilience and grace.

Finding balance also requires setting boundaries—honoring our limits and respecting our need for space and solitude. In a world that glorifies busyness and productivity, it's all too easy to become overwhelmed by the demands of work and personal obligations. But by establishing clear boundaries and prioritizing our well-being, we create the space for rest, reflection, and renewal. Like a sturdy fence that protects a garden from intruders, boundaries safeguard our time and energy, allowing us to cultivate a life of balance and harmony.

Moreover, achieving balance involves integrating work, personal life, and play in a way that honors our values and priorities. It's about finding synergy between our professional aspirations, personal relationships, and leisure pursuits, so that each aspect of our lives complements and enriches the others. Like a well-conducted orchestra, finding balance requires us to harmonize the different elements of our lives, creating a symphony of fulfillment and joy.

In conclusion, finding balance is an ongoing journey—a sacred quest for equilibrium and wholeness in a world of constant motion and change. As you navigate the labyrinth of life, remember these words: "Balance is not something you find, it's something you create." By prioritizing self-care, setting boundaries, and integrating work, personal life, and play, you can cultivate a life that is balanced, harmonious, and deeply fulfilling.

Chapter 14

The Journey of Self-Discovery

Embarking on the journey of self-discovery is akin to setting sail on an odyssey into the depths of your own being—an adventure filled with twists and turns, revelations and epiphanies. This chapter serves as your compass, guiding you through the labyrinth of self-exploration and encouraging you to delve deep into your inner world to uncover the essence of your true self.

Self-discovery is not a destination to be reached, but rather a lifelong journey of exploration and revelation. It's about peeling back the layers of conditioning and expectation to reveal the radiant core of your authentic self—the person you were born to be, untethered by societal norms or external pressures. Like a sculptor chiseling away at a block of marble, self-discovery is a process of unveiling the masterpiece that lies within.

The journey of self-discovery begins with self-awareness—the foundation upon which all else is built. By cultivating mindfulness and presence, you become attuned to the nuances of your thoughts, emotions, and desires, gaining insight into the patterns that shape your life. Through introspection and reflection, you unravel the tapestry of your experiences, uncovering the threads of your truest self amidst the chaos of daily existence.

As you delve deeper into the recesses of your psyche, you may encounter aspects of yourself that have long lain dormant—dreams deferred, passions suppressed, truths untold. Embracing the journey of self-discovery means confronting these shadows with courage and compassion, shining the light of awareness into the darkest corners of your soul. Like a spelunker exploring a cavern, you venture into the depths of your own consciousness, unearthing hidden treasures and confronting long-buried fears.

Self-discovery is also a process of integration—a weaving together of the fragmented pieces of your identity into a cohesive whole. As you explore the various facets of your personality—the light and the shadow, the strengths and the weaknesses—you begin to embrace the fullness of your humanity. By honoring all aspects of yourself with love and acceptance, you pave the way for healing and wholeness, allowing the disparate parts of your being to come together in harmony and balance.

In the end, the journey of self-discovery is a quest for authenticity—the courage to stand in your truth, unapologetically and unabashedly. It's about embracing the unique tapestry of your life—the triumphs and the tribulations, the joys and the sorrows—and recognizing that each thread contributes to the rich tapestry of your existence. By embarking on this sacred journey, you reclaim the power to shape your own destiny, forging a path that is uniquely yours and yours alone.

As you venture forth on the journey of self-discovery, remember these words: "To know thyself is the beginning of wisdom." By delving deep into your inner world, embracing self-awareness, and honoring all aspects of your being, you unlock the door to a life of authenticity, fulfillment, and purpose. So let us set sail together on this wondrous odyssey, guided by the light of self-discovery, and may we emerge from the depths of our own souls, reborn and renewed, ready to embrace the adventure that lies ahead.

Chapter 15

Cultivating Joy in Everyday Life

In the hustle and bustle of modern existence, it's all too easy to overlook the simple joys that surround us—the gentle caress of a breeze, the warmth of a morning sunbeam, the laughter of a loved one. Yet, it is in these seemingly mundane moments that the true essence of life resides—the raw, unadulterated joy that infuses every breath, every heartbeat, every fleeting second.

Cultivating joy in everyday life is not about grand gestures or extravagant indulgences. It's about embracing the beauty of the present moment and finding solace in life's simplest pleasures. It's about savoring the taste of a ripe, juicy peach, feeling the softness of a petal beneath your fingertips, or losing yourself in the melody of a familiar song. In these moments of quietude and simplicity, we discover a wellspring of joy that flows endlessly from the depths of our being.

One of the keys to cultivating joy in everyday life is mindfulness—the practice of being fully present and engaged in the here and now. By slowing down and tuning in to our senses, we open ourselves up to the richness of the present moment, allowing joy to permeate every aspect of our experience. Whether it's the vibrant colors of a sunset or the gentle rhythm of our own breath, mindfulness invites us to bask in the beauty of the present moment, finding joy in the simple act of being alive.

Gratitude is another potent tool for cultivating joy in everyday life. By cultivating a spirit of gratitude, we train our minds to focus on the blessings that surround us rather than fixating on what is lacking. Whether it's expressing thanks for a delicious meal, a kind word, or a breathtaking sunset, gratitude opens our hearts to the abundance that is already present in our lives, inviting joy to flourish and grow.

Connection is also essential to cultivating joy in everyday life. By nurturing deep connections with others—whether it's through shared laughter, heartfelt conversation, or acts of kindness—we create a sense of belonging and community that enriches our lives immeasurably. Joy is contagious, and by sharing our happiness with others, we amplify its power and potency, creating a ripple effect of positivity that reverberates throughout the world.

Finally, cultivating joy in everyday life is about embracing the impermanence of existence and finding beauty in the fleeting moments that make up our lives. Life is a tapestry of moments—some joyful, some sorrowful, but all woven together to create the rich tapestry of our existence. By embracing each moment with open arms and an open heart, we open ourselves up to the full spectrum of human experience, allowing joy to permeate even the darkest corners of our souls.

So let us take a moment to pause, to breathe, and to savor the sweetness of life's simple pleasures. Let us cultivate joy in the everyday moments—the laughter of a child, the beauty of a flower, the warmth of a loving embrace. For it is in these moments that we discover the true richness of life, and it is in these moments that we find joy everlasting.

Chapter 16

Building Financial Well-being

In the grand tapestry of life, our financial well-being forms a crucial thread, woven intricately into the fabric of our overall happiness and fulfillment. While money alone cannot buy happiness, the way we manage our finances can profoundly impact our sense of security, freedom, and overall well-being. In this chapter, we delve into the relationship between financial health and personal fulfillment, offering guidance on how to build a solid foundation of financial well-being that aligns with our values and aspirations.

At its core, financial well-being is not just about accumulating wealth or material possessions—it's about cultivating a healthy relationship with money that supports our broader goals and values. It's about finding a balance between spending and saving, between enjoying the present and planning for the future, and between meeting our needs and pursuing our dreams.

One of the first steps in building financial well-being is gaining clarity about our values and priorities. By identifying what truly matters to us—whether it's supporting our family, pursuing our passions, giving back to our community, or achieving financial independence—we can align our financial decisions with our deepest aspirations, ensuring that our money serves as a tool for living a meaningful and fulfilling life.

Budgeting is another essential aspect of building financial well-being. By creating a clear and realistic budget that accounts for our income, expenses, and savings goals, we gain a greater sense of control and clarity over our finances. Budgeting allows us to track our spending, identify areas where we can cut back or reallocate resources, and prioritize our spending in a way that reflects our values and priorities.

Saving and investing are also integral components of financial well-being. By setting aside a portion of our income for savings and investments, we create a safety net for ourselves and our loved ones, ensuring that we have the resources to weather unexpected expenses or emergencies. Moreover, investing wisely can help us grow our wealth over time, allowing us to achieve our long-term financial goals and aspirations.

However, building financial well-being is not just about accumulating wealth—it's also about cultivating a mindset of abundance and gratitude. By practicing gratitude for the resources we have and adopting an abundance mindset that focuses on what is possible rather than what is lacking, we shift our relationship with money from one of scarcity and fear to one of abundance and empowerment.

Finally, building financial well-being requires us to cultivate habits of mindfulness and intentionality in our financial decisions. By being mindful of our spending habits, practicing delayed gratification, and making intentional choices about how we use our money, we can ensure that our financial decisions are aligned with our values and aspirations, leading to greater peace of mind and fulfillment.

In conclusion, building financial well-being is a journey—a journey that requires patience, discipline, and a willingness to align our financial decisions with our deepest values and aspirations. By gaining clarity about our priorities, creating a realistic budget, saving and investing wisely, cultivating a mindset of abundance, and practicing mindfulness and intentionality in our financial decisions, we can build a solid foundation of financial well-being that supports our overall happiness and fulfillment.

Chapter 17

The Role of Altruism in Personal Fulfillment

In the intricate dance of life, there exists a profound truth: the more we give, the more we receive. This chapter delves into the transformative power of altruism—the act of selflessly giving of oneself for the benefit of others—and how it enriches our lives with personal happiness and a profound sense of purpose.

At its core, altruism is a beacon of light, illuminating the path toward personal fulfillment and inner peace. When we extend a helping hand to others, whether through acts of kindness, volunteering, or philanthropy, we not only make a positive impact on their lives but also experience a deep sense of joy and fulfillment within ourselves.

One of the remarkable aspects of altruism is its ability to foster connections with others and cultivate a sense of belonging and community. When we engage in acts of kindness and generosity, we create bonds of empathy and compassion that transcend differences and unite us in a shared humanity. These connections nourish our souls, providing us with a sense of belonging and purpose that enriches our lives in profound ways.

Moreover, altruism has been scientifically proven to boost our overall well-being and happiness. Studies have shown that acts of kindness and generosity activate neural pathways in the brain associated with pleasure and reward, leading to an increased sense of happiness and fulfillment. Additionally, altruistic behavior has been linked to lower levels of stress, anxiety, and depression, as well as improved physical health and longevity.

Furthermore, engaging in acts of altruism provides us with a sense of meaning and purpose—a deeper understanding of our place in the world and our ability to make a positive difference. When we give back to others, whether through volunteering our time, donating to charity, or simply offering a listening ear, we tap into a wellspring of purpose that infuses our lives with meaning and significance.

It's important to note that altruism is not about grand gestures or extravagant displays of generosity—it's about the simple, everyday acts of kindness and compassion that we extend to those around us. Whether it's lending a helping hand to a neighbor in need, offering words of encouragement to a friend going through a tough time, or volunteering at a local charity, every act of kindness, no matter how small, has the power to create ripple effects of positivity and joy.

In conclusion, altruism is a powerful force for personal fulfillment and happiness—a beacon of light that illuminates the path toward a life of meaning and purpose. By extending acts of kindness and generosity to others, we not only make a positive impact on their lives but also experience profound joy and fulfillment within ourselves. As we embrace the transformative power of altruism, may we continue to sow seeds of kindness and compassion, knowing that the greatest gift we can give is the love and support we offer to others.

Chapter 18

Embracing Solitude for Growth

In the cacophony of modern life, amidst the bustling crowds and ceaseless chatter, there exists a sanctuary—an oasis of stillness and reflection known as solitude. This chapter delves into the profound benefits of embracing solitude for introspection, creativity, and personal growth, challenging the stigma that surrounds spending time alone.

Solitude, far from being a lonely exile, is a sacred space where we can retreat from the noise of the world and reconnect with our inner selves. It provides us with an opportunity for deep introspection, allowing us to explore our thoughts, emotions, and dreams without distraction or interruption. In the silence of solitude, we can listen to the whispers of our hearts, gaining insight into our deepest desires and aspirations.

Moreover, solitude is a fertile ground for creativity to flourish. When we free ourselves from the constant barrage of external stimuli, we create space for inspiration to strike, for ideas to germinate and take root. In the solitude of our own company, we can unleash our imagination, allowing it to roam freely and unfettered. Whether through writing, painting, or simply daydreaming, solitude offers us a canvas upon which to express ourselves in ways that are authentic and uninhibited.

Beyond its creative benefits, solitude is also a catalyst for personal growth and self-discovery. When we spend time alone, we confront our fears, insecurities, and doubts head-on, without the distractions of the outside world. In the solitude of self-reflection, we gain clarity and perspective, understanding ourselves more deeply and authentically. Solitude provides us with the space to heal old wounds, to nurture our spirits, and to cultivate resilience in the face of life's challenges.

It's important to recognize that solitude is not synonymous with loneliness. While loneliness is a state of isolation and disconnection from others, solitude is a conscious choice—a deliberate retreat into the sanctuary of our own company. It is a time of self-care and self-nurturing, a gift we give ourselves to replenish our spirits and nourish our souls.

In a society that often equates solitude with loneliness and isolation, it's time to challenge the stigma surrounding spending time alone. Solitude is not a weakness to be avoided or feared but a strength to be embraced and celebrated. By embracing solitude, we unlock a treasure trove of inner wisdom and creativity, fostering personal growth and self-discovery in ways we never thought possible.

In conclusion, solitude is a sacred space—a sanctuary of stillness and reflection where we can reconnect with our inner selves, unleash our creativity, and foster personal growth. By challenging the stigma surrounding spending time alone, we empower ourselves to embrace solitude as a powerful tool for introspection, creativity, and self-discovery. As we journey into the depths of solitude, may we find solace, inspiration, and renewal, knowing that the greatest adventures await those who dare to venture into the quiet recesses of their own souls.

Chapter 19

Navigating Life's Transitions

Life is a journey filled with twists and turns, peaks and valleys, and moments of profound change. In this chapter, we explore strategies for smoothly navigating life's inevitable transitions, viewing them not as obstacles to be feared but as opportunities for growth and renewal.

Transitions are an inherent part of the human experience—whether it's starting a new job, moving to a new city, or experiencing a major life event such as marriage or parenthood. While transitions can be daunting and unsettling, they also present us with opportunities for growth, self-discovery, and transformation.

The key to navigating life's transitions lies in embracing change with an open heart and a resilient spirit. Instead of resisting the inevitable, we can choose to lean into the unknown, trusting that change brings with it the seeds of new beginnings and fresh possibilities. By reframing transitions as opportunities for growth and renewal, we empower ourselves to embrace change as a natural and necessary part of the journey of life.

One of the most effective strategies for navigating life's transitions is to cultivate a mindset of flexibility and adaptability. Rather than clinging to the familiar and the comfortable, we can learn to embrace the uncertainty of change, recognizing that it is often in times of transition that we experience the most profound growth and transformation. By remaining open to new possibilities and willing to adapt to changing circumstances, we can navigate life's transitions with grace and resilience.

Another important aspect of navigating life's transitions is to practice self-care and self-compassion. Transitions can be emotionally and physically draining, leaving us feeling vulnerable and overwhelmed.

During times of transition, it's crucial to prioritize our well-being and to be gentle with ourselves as we navigate the challenges and uncertainties that lie ahead. By practicing self-care and self-compassion, we can replenish our spirits, recharge our energy, and approach life's transitions with renewed strength and resilience.

Furthermore, seeking support from others can be invaluable during times of transition. Whether it's leaning on friends and family for emotional support, seeking guidance from mentors or counselors, or connecting with support groups of individuals who are going through similar experiences, reaching out to others can provide us with the encouragement and reassurance we need to navigate life's transitions with confidence and courage. By surrounding ourselves with a supportive community, we can draw strength from the collective wisdom and resilience of those around us.

In conclusion, life's transitions are inevitable, but they need not be feared. By embracing change with an open heart and a resilient spirit, by cultivating flexibility, self-care, and support from others, we can navigate life's transitions with grace and courage. Rather than viewing transitions as obstacles to be overcome, we can see them as opportunities for growth, renewal, and transformation. As we journey through life's transitions, may we embrace the unknown with curiosity and optimism, trusting that each new chapter holds the promise of new beginnings and endless possibilities.

Chapter 20

Reflections and Moving Forward

As we come to the final chapter of our transformative journey through "The Life You're Meant to Live: Paths to Purpose and Fulfillment," it's a time for reflection and contemplation. Throughout this book, we've embarked on a profound exploration of self-discovery, growth, and the pursuit of a life filled with meaning and joy. Now, as we bring our journey to a close, let us take a moment to reflect on the insights gained and consider how we can continue our path of growth, exploration, and fulfillment beyond the pages of this book.

First and foremost, let us acknowledge the courage and commitment it takes to embark on a journey of self-discovery and personal growth. It's not always easy to confront our fears, challenge our limiting beliefs, and step out of our comfort zones. Yet, by taking that first step, by opening our hearts and minds to the possibilities within us, we've laid the foundation for a life filled with purpose and fulfillment.

As we reflect on the journey we've undertaken, let us celebrate the progress we've made and the insights we've gained along the way. Perhaps we've discovered new passions and interests, overcome long-held fears and doubts, or forged deeper connections with ourselves and others. Whatever the case may be, let us honor the growth and transformation that has taken place within us, recognizing that each step forward brings us closer to living the life we were truly meant to live.

Moving forward, let us commit to applying the insights and lessons learned from this journey to our daily lives. Whether it's embracing authenticity, cultivating gratitude, or nurturing deep connections with others, let us integrate these practices into our routines and interactions, knowing that small actions taken consistently over time can lead to profound shifts in our lives.

Moreover, let us remain open to the possibilities that lie ahead, knowing that the journey of self-discovery and personal growth is ongoing. Life is a constant process of learning, evolving, and becoming, and there will always be new challenges to overcome, new opportunities to seize, and new horizons to explore. As we continue our journey, let us approach each day with curiosity, courage, and an open heart, knowing that the greatest adventures await those who dare to follow their dreams.

In closing, I invite you to take a moment to envision the life you desire— the life filled with purpose, passion, and fulfillment. What steps can you take today to move closer to that vision? What practices can you incorporate into your daily life to cultivate joy, meaning, and connection? As you embark on this next chapter of your journey, remember that the power to create the life you desire lies within you. Trust in your inner wisdom, follow your heart, and embrace the journey with open arms and an open mind.

Thank you for accompanying me on this transformative journey. May you continue to grow, evolve, and live the life you were truly meant to live. And may your path be filled with love, joy, and endless possibilities.

"The Life You're Meant to Live: Paths to Purpose and Fulfillment" unfolds as a profound exploration into the essence of what it means to lead a life of deep significance and happiness. Through its pages, readers embark on a journey of self-discovery, unearthing the layers of their being to uncover a life rich in purpose and joy. This exploration delves into the complexities of human existence, offering insights and practical guidance to navigate the path toward a fulfilling life. It is a testament to the power of self-awareness, resilience, and connection in shaping our destinies.

The Beacon of Purpose

At the core of this journey is the quest for purpose—a beacon guiding us toward a life of fulfillment. The book asserts that discovering one's purpose is not merely an act of introspection but a dynamic process of engagement with the world. It emphasizes the importance of aligning one's actions with intrinsic values and passions, transforming everyday choices into steps toward a greater goal. The narrative weaves through personal stories and philosophical musings to illuminate the path to self-discovery, encouraging readers to reflect on their unique contributions to the world.

The Pillars of Fulfillment

The chapters serve as milestones in the journey toward understanding and embracing the multifaceted nature of fulfillment. Mindfulness, gratitude, and altruism are highlighted as essential practices that enrich our lives and the lives of those around us. The book underscores the significance of cultivating deep connections with others, pursuing our passions, and embracing authenticity as pathways to true happiness.

Mindfulness is presented as a tool for cultivating present-moment awareness, enabling us to experience life more fully and navigate its challenges with grace. The practice of gratitude is extolled for its power to shift perspectives, fostering a sense of abundance and contentment. Altruism is explored as a profound source of fulfillment, revealing that in giving to others, we find deeper meaning and satisfaction in our own lives.

Navigating Life's Challenges

The text acknowledges the inevitability of adversity and change, offering wisdom on cultivating resilience and flexibility. It addresses the art of embracing change as an opportunity for growth and self-renewal, emphasizing the importance of resilience in overcoming life's obstacles. Through personal anecdotes and psychological insights, the book provides strategies for transforming challenges into catalysts for transformation.

Financial well-being is discussed as a crucial aspect of a fulfilling life, not for the pursuit of wealth itself, but for the freedom and security it offers. The book advocates for a mindful approach to financial management, emphasizing the importance of aligning financial decisions with personal values and goals.

The Journey of Self-Discovery

Central to the book's message is the concept of self-discovery as a lifelong quest. It champions the virtues of solitude for introspection and creativity, arguing that in silence, we hear the most profound truths of our hearts. The narrative encourages readers to embrace their individuality, highlighting that authenticity is the foundation upon which a meaningful life is built.

Empowering Reflections

As the book draws to a close, it invites readers to reflect on their journey and the insights gained. It encourages a forward-looking perspective, emphasizing the importance of intentionality in crafting a life that resonates with one's deepest aspirations. The final chapters serve as a call to action to live with purpose, courage, and an open heart, inspiring readers to continue their journey of growth and fulfillment beyond the pages of the book.

Conclusion

"The Life You're Meant to Live: Paths to Purpose and Fulfillment" stands as a beacon for those seeking to navigate the complexities of life with wisdom and grace. It is a comprehensive guide that intertwines philosophical insights with practical advice, illuminating the path to a life of joy, purpose, and deep connection. Through its exploration of mindfulness, resilience, altruism, and the power of self-discovery, the book offers a transformative perspective on the art of living fully. It reminds us that fulfillment is not a distant dream but a journey that unfolds with each mindful step we take toward embracing our true selves and the world around us. In doing so, it invites us to embark on the most significant adventure of all—the quest to live the life we are truly meant to live.

Reflections for a Life of Purpose and Fulfillment: Inspirational Quotations from 'The Life You're Meant to Live

- "In the pursuit of purpose, every step taken with intention illuminates the path to fulfillment."
- "Embrace the journey of self-discovery like a river flowing to the sea; it knows not the obstacles, only the destination."
- "Resilience is the art of navigating life's storms with the grace of a dancer, turning each challenge into a step in the dance of life."
- "Mindfulness is the canvas where the moments of our lives are painted with the colors of awareness, making each day a masterpiece."
- "Gratitude is the lens through which the abundance of life comes into focus, transforming what we have into enough and more."
- "Altruism weaves the fabric of community, binding us with threads

of compassion that strengthen the tapestry of humanity."

- "Solitude is not the absence of noise, but the presence of peace, a sacred space for the soul to speak its truths."
- "Change is the sculptor of our character, chiseling away at the excess, revealing the masterpiece within."
- "In the heart of every challenge lies a lesson in disguise, waiting to unfold into wisdom for the journey ahead."
- "Financial well-being is not measured by wealth alone but by the freedom it grants to pursue what truly matters."
- "Authenticity is the bravest form of rebellion; living true to oneself is the ultimate expression of freedom."
- "The tapestry of life is richest when woven with diverse threads of experiences, challenges, and triumphs."
- "To navigate life's transitions is to dance with change, moving with its rhythm, leading with our dreams."
- "Joy is found not in the destination but in the beauty of the journey, in the simple pleasures that sprinkle our days with light."
- "Intentionality in action is like a compass for the soul, guiding our steps toward a life of purpose and passion."